Make Me An Offer

A Guidebook for Small Business Buyers and Sellers

By Larry Goldstein

ISBN 978-0-578-66896-3

Published by Fight On Publishing.

Connect with Larry Goldstein at

larryg@lvbusinessbroker.com

www.lvbusinessbroker.com

Table of Contents

_____

Dedication

This book is dedicated to my father, Dr. Raymond Goldstein, and my grandfather, Michael Kaplan. I am grateful for their love and teachings on living an exemplary life.

Preface

This guidebook was created to help small business buyers and sellers discover important considerations and actions to successfully buy or sell a business. I have included my personal business experiences to prompt reflection on your own business goals, leading you on the path to achieve your dream of buying or selling a small business.

I was intrigued by business at an early age and developed a perspective that was shaped by two people with very different lines of work. My first introduction to business at the age of five was when I joined my grandfather on trips to purchase shoes from wholesalers for his retail business. My attention was focused on selecting various styles from racks of samples while intensely listening to price negotiations. How captivating for a youngster!

As a middle schooler, I began to observe my father's business as a practicing dentist. It gave me valuable insight into the demands and rewards of an independent medical professional. I saw the freedom of self-employment weighed against the discipline required to wear multiple hats in order to be successful as a business owner.

I purchased an existing business in 2011 and focused on "running" my business to increase sales, ensure a high level of customer service, improve operational efficiencies, and use key performance indicators (KPIs) to identify deficiencies and measure results.

Just as important, I focused on strengthening certain subjective qualities that became the hallmark of how I "represented" myself and my business. These qualities included developing and maintaining long-term customer relationships, treating all customers and employees with integrity, never losing my temper in front of customers and employees, and deeply caring about the reputation of my business.

By the time I sold my business in 2016, revenues had more than doubled, customer numbers had greatly increased, a new brand had been created, mutual referrals had been established with business partners, and employee retention had stabilized.

All these undertakings ensured that my business was in order when I was ready to sell. It is imperative that a buyer sees themselves successfully running their new business from day one!

I began looking for the exit door the day I purchased my business with the goal to grow and sell in three to five years. Business owners may become overwhelmed by continually changing business conditions such as new competitors entering the marketplace, disruptive technologies being introduced, employee training required on an ongoing basis, and changing customer requirements.

These are just a few of what seems like an endless list of reasons why business owners may look for a way out. The daily demands of running a business may become consuming, but the primary goal must be kept top of mind: to prepare the business with the mindset of a "buyer" to achieve the maximum valuation.

The question I am asked by sellers most often is, "What is my business worth?" The pragmatic and economic answer is, "The price a ready, willing, and able buyer will pay." However, price tells little about the condition and future of a business. This guidebook provides insight into the process and key considerations to successfully buy or sell a small business.

Introduction

Buying or selling a business is a unique experience and requires a high level of planning and due diligence.

A business is like a living thing. It has its own distinct personality, abilities, challenges, and potential. More importantly, a business is like a child to its owner. It demands total commitment, attention, and management. It constantly requires planning for the future.

A business is not a commodity like a house or other possession. It is usually made up of many moving parts that are in constant motion, changing day by day. Ask anyone who has operated a business and they will most likely tell you that owning and operating a business is one of the most intense experiences. It can take over a person's life.

But owning and operating a business can provide great benefits: a purpose in life, a leadership role, a chance to test one's abilities in the marketplace of competition and ideas, a superior income, and, if done properly, a level of freedom and prestige that is otherwise hard to obtain in most professions[1] (see Fig. 1).

---

[1] Higley, Danielle. "More Money, More Family Time: Survey Reveals Why Self-employment is so Popular Right Now." Quickbooks Intuit.

In the United States, it is almost a "rite of passage" for people to contemplate going into business for themselves. This observation is particularly true for people who have obtained certain skills while acting as an employee for others. Some call it a "mid-life crisis," but others say that it is a call or challenge to test one's potential to become a proactive player in society and discover if one can take more control over one's life.

What is the most rewarding thing about working for yourself?

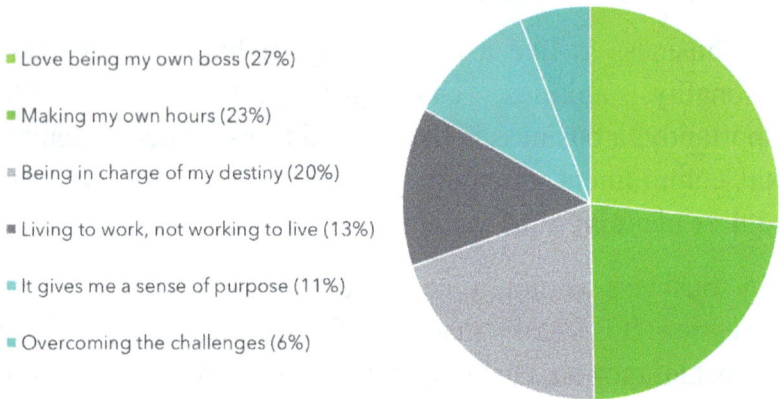

- Love being my own boss (27%)
- Making my own hours (23%)
- Being in charge of my destiny (20%)
- Living to work, not working to live (13%)
- It gives me a sense of purpose (11%)
- Overcoming the challenges (6%)

Figure 1. A summary of the benefits of being self-employed. Quickbooks Intuit. Accessed February 15, 2020. https://quickbooks.intuit.com/r/freelancer/self-employed-work-life-balance-survey/

On the other hand, many businesses get started by chance. In fact, over the past few decades, many highly skilled and ambitious people have been forced into starting their own business after an employer event such as bankruptcy, change of ownership, or downsizing.

---

https://quickbooks.intuit.com/r/freelancer/self-employed-work-life-balance-survey/ (accessed February 15, 2020).

For many middle-aged former employees, going into business is forced upon them… and they seize the moment. But for most, owning and operating their own business is a life-altering experience. When the "buck stops with you," and you take that responsibility seriously, you can be consumed by the demands of being the ultimate decision-maker.

Each year, there are over 20 million new business startups. Sadly, about 90% of new companies won't make it past the fifth year. But once a person has become a business owner, going back to being an employee again is not an acceptable option for most. Those who are not in the 10% don't just disappear from the game. No. Many become serial entrepreneurs once they realize that owning and operating a business is not that much of a mystery and isn't all that scary either.

It's a well-known fact that failure is just part of the experience for most successful business owners. It comes with the territory. Indeed, operating a successful business is not brain surgery and is not a skill that certain people are born with. In a way, it can be like learning how to ride a bicycle or drive a car. Experience is a great teacher, and just about anyone with some common sense, organizational skills, and a strong desire can become a successful business owner.

The Purpose of this Guide

Each year in the United States, over 10,000 small businesses—made up of 15 employees or less—participate in a buy–sell transaction[2] (see Fig. 2). And those are only the recorded transactions.

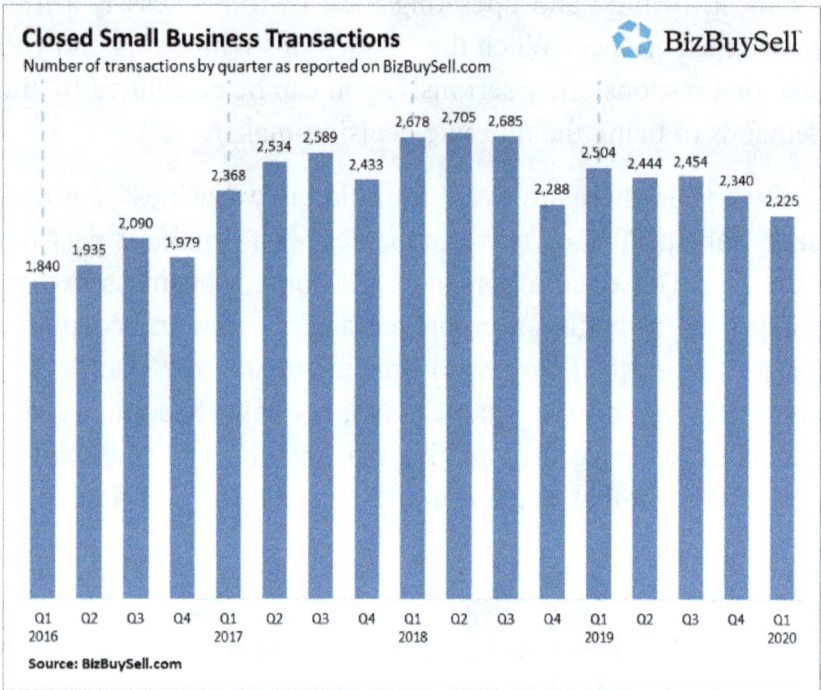

Closed Small Business Transactions
Number of transactions by quarter as reported on BizBuySell.com

BizBuySell

Q1 2016: 1,840
Q2: 1,935
Q3: 2,090
Q4: 1,979
Q1 2017: 2,368
Q2: 2,534
Q3: 2,589
Q4: 2,433
Q1 2018: 2,678
Q2: 2,705
Q3: 2,685
Q4: 2,288
Q1 2019: 2,504
Q2: 2,444
Q3: 2,454
Q4: 2,340
Q1 2020: 2,225

Source: BizBuySell.com

Figure 2. Number of closed small business transactions per quarter. BizBuySell. Accessed February 15, 2020. https://www.bizbuysell.com/insight-report/

It's estimated that at least twice that amount of transactions take place under the radar. Many of these "shadow transactions" take place in the For Sale by Owner (FSBO) market. This taxation-avoidance strategy can make it very problematic if these off-the-books transactions turn up major issues, such as when the new buyer finds out they have

---

[2] BizBuySell. "BizBuySell Insight Report." https://www.bizbuysell.com/insight-report/ (accessed February 15, 2020).

assumed all the former company's unknown debt or tax liabilities and "bad will" reputation.

Even more concerning when buying or selling a small business is the process of establishing the value of a company. It's an unfortunate truth that the vast majority of small businesses are operated very casually and do not use a formalized accounting system. Owning a small business is one of the most popular forms of "creative tax avoidance" when looking at how expenses are defined (more on that later). There are ways to work with this informal situation, but it takes a certain level of expertise and knowledge of the process to properly value a business. However, with that in mind, the real value of a company is determined when the owner and seller agree on a price.

Each business buy–sell transaction has a story behind it, and being able to understand that context and what it might mean to each party is another area that requires some special expertise. For example, many businesses go up for sale because of the lack of profitability. The lack of profits can be due to three main reasons:

1) The owner-operator is not a competent manager.

2) The market has changed and profit margins have eroded to the point of low or no profit.

Both of these common selling scenarios can offer a great opportunity in the hands of the right buyer who can identify the potential solutions to the problems a business is facing.

3) Owner-operator burnout. If the owner-operator cannot build an organization where duties can be reliably delegated, the owner-operator becomes a micro-manager and has to be involved in every little task, but eventually can't keep up the

pace. The owner-operator becomes just another overworked employee, and their life can become a nightmare dominated by the voracious demands of the business.

While these are the most common reasons for selling, there are many other factors that motivate a business owner to sell (or buy). Knowing what factors to consider is an essential aspect of making the right purchase.

This book will cover many of the important topics that should be considered when buying or selling a business. While we may not dive deeply into all the considerations, the goal of the book is to provide an introduction to the process of buying or selling a business and discuss why certain expertise is required to make sure this major transaction is done properly. Buying or selling a business is a complex process that requires specific knowledge and skills. Reinventing this wheel is normally a costly undertaking.

Chapter 1

Reasons for Selling a Business

While there are as many reasons for selling as there are business owners, the following is an overview of the most common.

1. Death or Incapacitation of the Owner-Operator

We are currently in an era where the post-World War II baby boomer generation is moving on to the "Great Beyond." Most commonly, small business owners of that generation were sole proprietors where they functioned as the center of responsibility and purposely constrained the growth of the company mainly to provide a living wage and standard of living for themselves and their families. Most were considered "owner-employees." They believed that growing the company usually meant either having a partner or hiring expensive administrative personnel as well as adding stress caused by dealing with too many employees and getting overly involved in their needs and personalities.

Additionally, in this type of "mom-and-pop" or family business, the original owner-operator typically has not planned for a transition of management to either children or key staff.

As a result, when "the boss" goes down, so does the business. The surviving spouse normally does not have enough knowledge to run the business and ends up putting the business up for sale or looks for other similar companies that might want to buy the company. Death of a spouse or parent can be a traumatic event, and the surviving spouse or family may act too hastily and may not understand the true value of the company.

In this situation, the most common reaction is to turn to the family attorney or other trusted individual, but that solution has the same potential flaws—lack of experience needed in order to carry out the due diligence required to facilitate such a transaction.

2. Owner-Operator Burnout

The genesis of most small, service-related businesses happens when a competent, skilled employee reaches the stage where they feel they can go into business for themselves. They know how to perform in a particular industry and they know the customer well. So, they strike out on their own, usually taking some key customers from the former employer.

If they are highly skilled and can attract and retain customers, they can build a successful business and possibly provide employment opportunities for others as well. Each town in America is loaded with these small businesses that play an important part in the everyday lives of thousands of communities. However, success can often run into a roadblock and potentially dangerous trap.

As the business grows, the owner-operator needs to hire more employees to handle the results of that growth. As more employees come on board, the costs of operations increase and it becomes harder to make sure the company can continue to deliver the same level of service and quality that attracted customers and brought the increasing revenue.

Soon, the owner-operator realizes that they aren't able to sufficiently supervise the operations to make sure each job is being done properly. They may try to delegate tasks to trusted employees, but unless properly compensated, many employees don't want the added responsibility of managing staff and handling customers.

The owner-operator may then become a micro-manager, having to be involved in too many business-related activities. Because they love their business or see it as a real test of their abilities, they begin to spend almost all their time deeply involved with the business operations. They are "alone at the top," and their personal life suffers to the point where they become miserable and beaten down.

The hope of being able to build an organization that has the infrastructure to allow owner-operators and management to delegate tasks and that uses managerial accounting for control and monitoring of daily operational performance is what usually keeps most successful small businesses from looking for buyers. Owner-operators want to regain a better quality of life. However, in fairness, being able to *do the business* is not the same thing as being able to *run and grow a business*. Most entrepreneurs may have the skills to do the job but have no training on how to operate and manage a business.

3. Lack of Profitability (Insufficient Cash Flow)

This situation usually runs in parallel with the owner-operator burnout, but not always. Many owner-operators have no business management training or understanding on how to use managerial accounting to monitor and hold the business accountable for performance. Most owners believe that a CPA or accountant is the go-to person to understand how the financial numbers correlate with business performance. But that is not the case.

CPAs and accountants are trained experts on "tax-based accounting," which is focused on how the financials of a company relate to what tax laws are applicable, and not how financial information relates to operations and profitability.

Managerial accounting is used by business managers to establish pricing, set budgets, measure employee productivity, establish goals, and set measurable objectives, particularly profit margins. Without at least some knowledge of managerial accounting, a business will miss key components of its financial picture.

Managerial accounting is not that difficult, but it is not in the interest of a CPA or accountant to advise on this matter as there are low-cost software tools (QuickBooks, Sage, or Peachtree, for example) that can provide all the information needed to operate a small company.

Managerial accounting starts with "engineering profit" based upon the actual expenses of the company. Most small, less-sophisticated businesses will set their pricing to what they see the market range is for their product or service. In reality, a company first needs to understand what it costs to provide the product or service before it can be properly priced.

Keep in mind that if a small company can cover all its costs and still have an extra 10% left over, that is considered a "good" profit margin (before paying taxes or interest). So, if the expenses are even just 10% above what the product or service is sold for, the company would make no profit. While this is a simplified example, you get the picture. Financial reports are as important to a manager as lab reports are to a physician.

A business must make a profit to survive, or eventually, it will run out of cash flow. This is a major reason why most small companies don't survive past the fifth year. But just running out of cash is not actually what happens in most cases.

Usually, before a company closes its doors, it has borrowed money from lenders, friends, or family, or it has sold off other assets. Thus, the actual demise starts when there is not enough profit to provide for **positive cash flow.**

Here is another factor to keep in mind. Most small companies—despite having an outsourced accountant—do not get regular, if even annual, financial reports. They only find out that there is no positive cash flow when they can't pay the bills, or worse, the payroll. (Unpaid payroll taxes is a serious problem and usually brings on the *coup de grace* from the IRS.)

4. Liquidation

In 2019, over 22,780 businesses filed for bankruptcy, and a good portion of those were forced to sell assets to satisfy their debts.[3] But not all businesses go through the costly process of bankruptcy, and instead, they self-liquidate before closing their doors. Sometimes, playing vulture can pay off for those who have experience operating a business.

---

[3] U.S. Bankruptcy Courts. "U.S. Bankruptcy Courts—Business and Nonbusiness Cases Commenced, by Chapter of the Bankruptcy Code, During the 12-Month Period Ending December 31, 2019." PDF file.
https://www.uscourts.gov/sites/default/files/data_tables/bf_f2_1231.2019.pdf (accessed February 15, 2020).

5. Transition Seekers

Here is an interesting and growing category. Similar to when the owner-operator passes away or becomes incapable of operating the business, this category involves an older generation of owners. However, here, these owners are actively looking to sell all or a portion of their successful business to the younger generation with the hopes that the successful ongoing business operations can pay a retirement income for the seller, who usually stays on as an advisor.

Typically, the owner-operator may have to go "head hunting" for a likely candidate, usually someone with experience in the industry. The owner sells a portion of the company equity to the candidate with the provision that the new partner will undergo a period of training and transition. Once the new partner has proven to be capable, the owner will sell more equity to the partner in exchange for a monthly retirement income.

6. Partial Equity Placement

Partial equity placement (PEP) is very similar to the transition seeker scenario we just covered. Some may refer to PEP as a "private placement," but it is not quite the same. A partial equity sale is one way a company can raise needed capital rather than acquiring debt through a loan. However, these types of offerings are particularly tricky, especially if the potential partner doesn't undertake the required due diligence or has no experience in the industry.

7. Make Me an Offer

Over the last few decades, corporate business consolidations, reorganizations, and relocations have had a profound effect on many experienced and well-paid middle managers. Often, these managers are too old to start again as a new employee elsewhere and have few options other than to go into business for themselves. On the plus side, many of them have business management expertise, as well as access to capital.

Under this scenario, the buyer may start out by looking for a business they wish to purchase, but that business may not yet be on the market. As the old saying goes, "Everything has its price." Many business owners have probably entertained the sale of their business many times but have not acted on it. So when a qualified and motivated buyer appears at their door, most owners would consider the sale. As a result, they ask the potential buyer to "make me an offer." With nothing to lose, the owners can always respectfully say, "No, thanks."

8. Partner Disputes

Business partnerships are life-changing relationships that require mutual trust and respect. Money is involved and a conscious choice must be made every day to work toward common goals.

Studies show that up to 70% of business partnerships fail and the complexity increases exponentially when multiple partners are involved.[4] Unfortunately, the last agreement between partners is a dissolution agreement.

This can sometimes present a good opportunity for a buyer if the partners are in a hurry to sell the business. Just be sure

---

[4] Ward, Susan. "Why Business Partnerships Fail." The Balance Small Business. https://www.thebalancesmb.com/why-business-partnerships-fail-4107045 (accessed February 15, 2020).

you understand the reasons behind the sale and that they don't have to do with any potential downfalls in the business itself.

Summary

As a buyer, always listen to the seller's reasons for selling, but also look beyond them for other reasons as this may help you identify the areas of the business that may be a struggle. Always keep in mind that sellers who make the decision to sell are typically already in the process of checking out of their business as well. They may be in a hurry, but you can't afford to be.

A business should be judged on its merits separate from the seller, or anything the seller is telling you regarding why they're selling. Take the time for due diligence so you are sure that you're making an educated buying decision.[5]

---

[5] Daoust, Mark. "The 7 Most Common Reasons People Give For Selling Their Business." Quiet Light Brokerage. https://www.quietlightbrokerage.com/7-common-reasons-people-sell-business/ (accessed February 15, 2020).

Chapter 2

Reasons for Buying a Business

Most people who are interested in owning a business want to gain some of the benefits that come with it; they want to be independent, make decisions, be the boss, and live a good life with a high-quality lifestyle. Owning a successful business is one way to achieve all of those things.

Since the end of World War II, when America was the only large economy left standing, the U.S. economy took off, and there were new domestic industries and a shortage of workers. That scenario created America's golden years. The cost of living was relatively inexpensive (in 1960, a new home cost $11,900, about the same as a nine-month apartment rental today). Employees made a good wage, and new social programs were in style. Unions, funded pensions, and upward mobility were all in full swing.

But, as with most things, change happened over time. For many reasons, workers slowly began to lose their upward financial and organizational mobility. As the day of the employee began its marginalization, the day of the entrepreneur started to come into being.

During the golden '50s, many employees were able to accumulate enough capital to go into business for themselves, and at the same time, there was a growing demand for more services. Over the recent past, risk-taking entrepreneurs have done very well filling the ever-growing services niche as well as taking many small businesses up to the level of medium-sized businesses and even public companies.

Today, many small service businesses can pay their owners much more income than highly educated employees earn in their employment. The reasons for that are outside the scope of this guide. However, the bottom line is that being a business owner can provide at least the promise of excellent living without the need to spend years and big dollars getting an advanced education or working for a high paying corporation. The potential to control one's destiny is still a siren's song to those with upward mobility aspirations.

As a child, I remember my father setting expectations to become a "professional." Armed with an engineering bachelor's degree and an MBA, I became a well-paid employee in the telecommunications industry. The dot-com crash of 2000 resulted in three "rightsizing" job changes in just nine years, and the flourishing days of my career nosedived. Becoming a business owner in 2011 enriched me with a broad set of business skills, absolute decision-making, high self-esteem, and financial security.

But that is just one story. The reasons why others decide to buy a business are plenty. Here is an overview of the six most common reasons.

1. Bypassing the Competition for High-Paying, "Secure" Corporate Jobs

It used to be that the way to the "good life" was through education, knowing the right people, and getting a secure job with a large corporation offering full benefits. Many capable corporate employees now dream of escaping corporate life and seek a more personalized, independent way to make a living; this is particularly true with stagnated corporate middle management. Changes in today's corporate workplace are driving employees to dream big and achieve entrepreneurship. Potential buyers can also find an ample supply of risk capital seeking a good way to make a return on investment.

The reality is that an annual salary of $60,000 for a one-worker-income family is barely enough to sustain a lower-middle-class lifestyle. With the current taxation system, employees in that tax bracket net a fairly skimpy take-home pay. Entrepreneurs have more opportunities to keep more of their income than a W-2 employee. This fact has become an incentive to many of our best minds who look to entrepreneurship as a way to optimize their social-economic life.

Middle-age business buyers are able to leverage their corporate experience and knowledge as it relates to running a business. They see where aspects of the business fit their experience, skills, and interests. While the income may not be the same as in the corporate environment, many ex-corporate executives will gladly trade the benefits of the corporate environment and its demands for those gained through entrepreneurship.

2. Securing an Income

Many buyers are just looking for a way to create a job for themselves. They don't care what type of business it is; they are all about the money-making potential. Even profitability is not as important as the cash flow that can be generated to at least pay the bills and sustain a reasonable way of life free from the politics of the workplace. One of the main advantages of buying an up-and-running enterprise is that it is already established and poses much less risk than putting capital into a startup business.

3. Merger and Acquisition

Successful companies can expand their brand and gain synergistic benefits by purchasing similar businesses. These buyers are more knowledgeable about the chosen industry and have an understanding of what to look for in a business. Location is typically the main motivator for this strategy no matter what financial condition the company may find itself. The acquiring company often will purchase the business and keep the ex-owner as an employee to continue operating the business.

4. The Hobbyist

Some buyers, particularly those with high net worth, like to purchase a business that they have an interest in or that operates in an area of personal passion they would like to pursue. For example, a hobbyist may be more interested in businesses in the fields of art, education, or sport. These folks are looking for something to keep them active and engaged in the community, and the financial aspects of the business may not play as important a part as with most buyers.

5. The Asset Buyer

On occasion, a buyer will not be interested in the business but more interested in the real estate the business occupies or the intellectual properties it may own. Additionally, and more commonly, a buyer may want the talent and services possessed by the seller. A good example is the current war for talent in the technical arena.

6. The Flipper

When the financial and real estate meltdown happened in 2008, the bubble burst on real estate prices for the first time in a generation. Not long after that, a new boom in real estate "flipping" came into being. Buy low, fix it up, and sell it at a good profit. The boom is playing on the most successful investing formula of all time: "buy low and sell high."

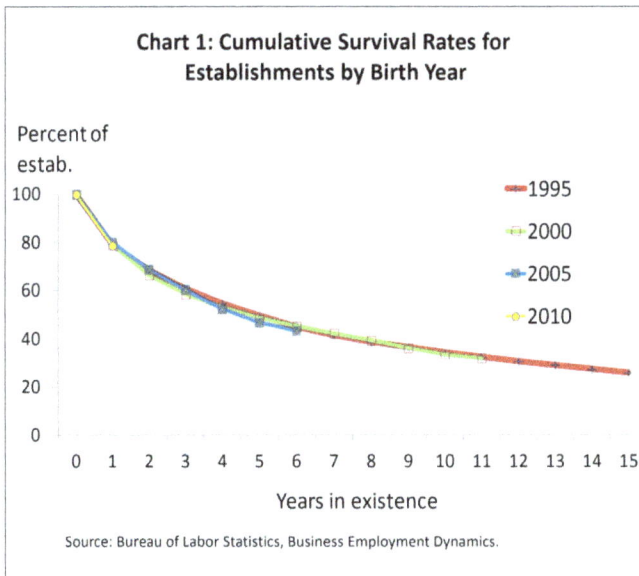

Figure 3. A chart showing cumulative survival rates for establishments by birth year. SBA Office of Advocacy. Accessed February 15, 2020.
https://www.sba.gov/sites/default/files/Business-Survival.pdf

As previously mentioned, over 90% of new businesses fail before reaching the fifth year[6] (see Fig. 3). Many of those businesses failed with the unintentional help from inexperienced owners and managers. However, many failing businesses can be turned into profitable ones, just like flipping real estate. Business flippers are usually well versed in management and finance.

Just as in the real estate market, business buyers in this category are looking for a "fixer-upper" to fix and flip.

Now it's time to go hunting for a business or a buyer. As you will see in the next section, buying or selling a business is different from most transactions. Indeed, when buying or selling a business, the transaction usually means immense changes in one's life.

---

[6] SBA Office of Advocacy. "Small Business Facts." PDF file. https://www.sba.gov/sites/default/files/Business-Survival.pdf (accessed February 15, 2020).

Chapter 3

Seller Due Diligence

Before considering the sale of a business, the seller needs to develop an action plan to be ready for the sale. The following list includes the most recommended steps to take to prepare for the sale of your business.

1. Analyze why you want to sell the business.

This question will surely come up in any discussions with a potential buyer. Above all, be honest with yourself. If you try to make up excuses and they do not sound credible, it will create an atmosphere of distrust with the potential buyer.

Another thing to consider is the seller's current state of health. Is he or she run down and tense? Are they depressed and do they worry about the future? Sometimes all they might need is a break or counseling. As they say, it is lonely at the top, and often it is difficult to share business problems with others, even a spouse.

2. Can you identify any fixes that might address why you feel the need to sell?

Sometimes, owners let their egos get the better of them, and this can nullify any attempts to seek outside help to analyze and fix problems within the company. While having consultants come into the business can be costly, consider allowing a business consultant determine whether the company can sustain growth-inducing activities. Owners often can't see how making some adjustments can improve cash flow, if that is indeed part of the problem. Too often, sellers accept that there is no salvation, and they end up being wrong.

3. What will the seller do once the business has been sold?

Of course, what you may do after the sale will depend on how much capital you have as the result of the sale. Importantly, the seller needs to have an idea of what they plan to do post-sale. Perhaps it's just to take a break and consider the future. Or selling the business may mean going back to being an employee for some people who may have found that their idea of owning and operating a business was different from reality.

4. Thoroughly investigate your post-sale options before deciding to sell.

Related to Step #3, a potential seller should seriously consider the impact of selling their company. Imagine yourself in your next work environment and how you and your family will live. Take the time to investigate the possibilities and how the sale may affect different areas of your life. Sometimes it appears that the grass is greener on the other side, but this is not always the case.

5. Carefully notify potential buyers that the business is for sale.

It's logical to give careful consideration about how to market the business. Customers may stop coming if they know the business is for sale. Vendors may become nervous if they find out about the potential sale as they may fear the business is in financial trouble and not able to pay for their services. The ownership may not want their reputation tarnished by the suggestion that the sale means they have failed. Employees may become nervous and start looking for new employment.

As a result, **the owner needs to be very discrete** when it comes to discussing the sale of the business.

First, the owner should think of who would be the most likely interested buyers. Are any competitors looking to expand in the area? Is there an industry association that can reach out to similar industry owners in out-of-town locations? Are any local companies closing in the area where some of the executives may be looking for alternative employment like starting their own business? These are some potential "low hanging fruit," but what if none of those opportunities present themselves?

The best way to keep the potential sale confidential and to maintain control of related communication is to work with a local business broker. They will guard the confidentiality as well as discretely market the enterprise offering, careful not to divulge the business or the seller's identity.

Also, they can help develop a local and national marketing plan and assist with creating the Sales Memorandum / Confidential Business Profile / Executive Summary. More importantly, the business broker can control who and when a potential buyer can visit the enterprise location and help deliver the due diligence documentation while the owner continues to run the business.

6. Put together a sales brochure (Confidential Business Profile) outlining the following:

    a. The nature of the business and industry

    b. How long the business has existed

    c. Description of the local market and competition

    d. Description of what differentiates the business from competitors

    e. Listing of any protected intellectual property

    f. Discussion of sales trends

    g. Description of operational assets

    h. Information about living in the local community (for non-local buyers)

    i. Reason for selling (consult with your business broker)

    j. Potential business expansion opportunities

7. Clean up the financial reports.

Financial reports are perhaps the most problematic area that needs attention. A very important thing to understand about the financials is the need to define **"total return to ownership."**

As an owner, the company probably pays your salary, your FICA, FUTA, and SUTA taxes, perhaps your car payment, gas, entertainment, and travel expenses, and maybe your insurance as well as any bonuses. All of these items are benefits to the owner. These items or portions of them should be added to any profits (or losses). The total return to ownership demonstrates the cash flow the company operations can generate. The use of a total return to owner (also known as Seller's Discretionary Cash Flow or SDCF) is particularly important when the company has a "pass-through" capability such as in the case with a sole proprietorship, S corporation, or LLC corporate structure.

Because small, private company financials are notorious for errors and omissions, many buyers will not consider the profits as shown in the operating statement. Instead, they prefer to base the valuation of the company on recorded sales. They do this because most states have a sales tax requirement that must be reported and paid quarterly under penalty of legal action by the state. A potential buyer can use the sales tax reports to help substantiate recorded sales. Normally, you will need at least the last three or four years of operating statements and balance sheets, which will show trends over several years.

Franchised businesses also provide a potential buyer with sales and royalty records, further ensuring credibility of the financial records. Franchises often sell faster due to reliable sales records, franchisor support, and established procedures.

8. Gather and organize your POS records.

In addition to other business records, a potential buyer will want to see the company's sales records. If the business uses a POS (point-of-sale) system, you can easily gather copies of all month-end summary reports. The reports should be filed in monthly order. From an operational point of view, the POS records are one of the most valuable assets to have for a new owner.

9. Clean up the location, equipment, and operations.

It's not unusual during times of stress and mismanagement to let the business lose its luster. The irony is that polishing up the business may be an opportunity to find solutions to whatever has been ailing the company. Making the business look sharp and functioning well can have an important, positive effect on qualified buyers and the ultimate sale price. Normally, before making a purchase, potential buyers will visit the location several times, either as secret shoppers or by just "cruising by" to check out the business location.

10. Gather all required documentation.

Make sure you have all required documents, including the following:

a. Articles of Incorporation

b. Business license

c. Insurance policies

d. Property mortgage or lease agreement

e. Fire and OSHA inspection reports

f. Equipment, services, and other contractual agreements

g. Health department certification (if required)

h. Any special authorizations or exceptions

11. Gather any employee handbook, policies and procedures, training program documentation, and employee reviews.

Many small businesses do not have many of these types of company documents. Well-managed companies will have these documents in place as an important part of daily operations. Not having these policies and practices can leave a company vulnerable to lawsuits and labor law violations. Indeed, having video training for employees can be a very valuable asset in the valuation of a business. Training videos for high employee turnover industries such as restaurants and retail shops are particularly useful.

12. Finance the pre-sale effort.

When companies are put up for sale due to poor financial performance, it may be difficult for sellers to pay for the suggested pre-sale preparation, as described throughout this section. Some facilities may help finance the small amount needed to prepare the business for sale. Often, the financing can be secured by equipment or even a guarantee of payment upon the sale of the business. If this is a problem, talk with your business broker; many local communities are very interested in the health of their business community.

13. Coordinate with your business broker.

Once the pre-sale due diligence is complete, coordinate the start of the sale with a planned campaign. One of the main tasks of the business broker is to be the "gatekeeper" and qualifier for all leads. The job of the owner-operator is to run the business and let the broker handle the sales process.

During this phase of the process, it is important to be discrete about the impending sale. When the actual sales process starts, the broker and owner-operator need to coordinate their communication so that employees do not become suspicious. For example, broker–client meetings should be held away from the business. Of course, any serious buyers will want to visit the location during operations, and this should be done as anonymously as possible.

Chapter 4

Buyer Due Diligence

There is a range of types of business buyers. Some experienced buyers know the industry and the type of business they wish to purchase. Often, these buyer candidates will try to approach the owner-operator directly as they are familiar with the type of business and the buy–sell process.

There are also buyers who have experience owning and operating a business and are looking for a business that they have an interest in but have no real experience within that industry.

Finally, there are buyers who are looking for a source of income and may know little or nothing about owning and operating a business. No matter what the situation, there is a basic due diligence process that should be followed by each potential buyer.

1. Understand why you are looking to purchase a business rather than find a job.

If you are hoping that owning and operating a business will give you an easier, less complicated work life or career, don't be deceived! When you are an employee, it's easy to leave work behind at the end of each day. Not so as an owner. Most of your waking hours will be dedicated to examining and analyzing all aspects of the business, the economy, and your customers.

To be a successful owner-operator, it takes a level of engagement and commitment way beyond that of an employee. Indeed, as an owner, at least until a structured organization is created, your lifestyle will always revolve around the business. Free time and extracurricular activities will most likely take a back seat to the business.

Your desired level of involvement in the daily operations of the business as an absentee owner or owner-operator is a major factor in the search for a business. The type of business, existing management capabilities, and competitive landscape all play a large determination of the necessity of direct owner involvement to ensure success.

   a. Make a list of requirements and benefits you expect to derive from owning your own business.

   b. Make a list of the time commitment and activities you are prepared to commit to such as travel, community involvement, and business-to-business (B2B) networking.

   c. Make a list of things you think will make you a good owner-operator, as well as a list of things you feel you may struggle with as a business owner.

   d. Determine your risk tolerance for the required financial investment and expected returns.

2. If you know what type of business you wish to purchase, research everything you can about the industry, its history, and its potential future outlook.

Even better, visit the type of business you are interested in owning and talk with the owner. (If they try to sell you their business, run for the door.) Ask them what they like and don't like about the business. Ask them what they see as the most important aspect of running the business.

If the owner seems willing, ask them if you could observe their operations and ask some questions. Don't just imagine what owning and operating a business would be like. Try to understand what it is like from someone who is actually living it.

3. If you are not sure about what business you are interested in, revisit your reasons for thinking about purchasing a business.

    a. If you are looking for income potential, research what types of businesses can provide the best return on investment.

    b. If you are looking for an escape from the corporate setting but want to be able to delegate daily operational tasks, look for businesses that already have an organizational setup with experienced employees.

    c. If you are looking for a lifestyle change, analyze what type of business will fit the type of lifestyle you wish to live, but harshly examine whether that business can provide the income needed for your desired lifestyle. To do that, you need to have a firm grasp on your personal budget.

d. If you have absolutely no idea of how to go about searching for a business, make contact with a business broker. They will know what types of businesses are on the market and can help you discover what types of businesses might work with your desired goals in business ownership. A business broker can also provide an explanation of how different businesses function from an ownership perspective. Like everything else, owning a business has its pros and cons. If it were easy to own and operate a business, everyone would be doing it.

4. Is your significant other ready for the type of commitment and potential risks of owning a business, as they will also be along for the ride?

Owning and operating a business will have an impact on your private life. If there is strife in an important relationship, it can become a real distraction for the owner-operator. If your significant other will be part of the operations of the company, realize that it can also put a strain on the relationship.

5. Find out if the business has a Sales Memorandum.

Determine if the business has a sales memorandum that describes the history of the business, its customers, competition, and reason for selling. The sale price should not be a big concern at this point until you find out more about the business's current situation.

That said, one of the first things you and a business broker should do is understand what level of capital is required for various types of businesses and which ones may fit into your financial reality.

6. If the business has a website, check it out and research any local competitors.

Check for the website page rank and visitors per day. Additionally, perform research to locate the potential local competition and see how their site ranks as well.

7. Google the business and a map of its location as well as the locations of nearby competitors.

For most retail businesses, location is very important. Is it located on a busy street? You can get a count for the vehicles per day from the state or city department of transportation. You can also find commercial rental prices online and see how many businesses might be listed for sale in the area.

8. Research the local demographics.

City-data.com is one online resource that provides a plethora of information for most cities in America. At a minimum, some key factors to consider are the following:

    a. Population and growth trends

    b. Per capita income

    c. Employment rate and trends

    d. Median household income

    e. Median ages and a breakdown of age ranges

f. Profile of local businesses

g. Building construction and housing stats

h. Crime statistics

i. Municipalities

j. Any other data that might apply to potential customers

9. Contact relevant business associations.

Many industries have national and regional associations made up of business owners as members. The associations typically have knowledgeable industry staff to provide industry education. Normally, these associations publish monthly industry magazines. They also organize and host national and regional events and webinars.

10. Contact local Chamber of Commerce offices.

Almost every city has a chapter of the Chamber of Commerce, which is made up of local business owners and managers. This group can also offer resources and a general view of the local business climate as well as local municipal business initiatives.

11. Contact local business development offices.

Many cities have local business development representatives who are charged with trying to develop the local economy and recruit new businesses into the area. Some cities may offer incentives for new businesses by offering things such as tax relief and valuable information on city planning as well as what is happening in the local business community. However, keep in mind that these folks are interested in recruiting and may be a bit biased about their communities.

12. Prepare to approach a potential business acquisition.

Things can get interesting when you decide to move forward. They can also be a bit delicate. As mentioned in the section on the seller's due diligence requirements, being discrete about the sale of a business is very important. As a result, it is difficult to know which business may actually be on the market; this is where a local business broker comes in.

Business brokers are not only a principal point of contact for discrete advertising of a business for sale, but, more importantly, business brokers act as advisers during the entire sales process. Yes, they do work on a commission, based mainly on the sale price, but their knowledge of the market and ability to coordinate and negotiate are great assets well worth the service.

Remember, the owner needs to be focused on running the business and not be distracted by the many steps of the sale process. In fact, just being able to have a third party do the negotiations makes the process easier and run so much smoother with a higher probability of success. When negotiating face to face between buyer and seller, emotions can get in the way. By having a third-party negotiator, offers and counteroffers can be made without the implications of "face-saving" or the subtle negative communication through body language.

Also, many documents need to be gathered and distributed to other professional participants in such a transaction and having an agent responsible for "cat herding" the paperwork and making sure all the details are taken care of provides great value and helps to preserve the confidentiality of the sale.

13. Qualify as a potential buyer.

One of the first things buyers want to know is "what's the price?" But purchasing a business is not like buying something off the shelf or even a larger transaction like purchasing a home. Sellers do not want to waste time on "tire kickers" or take a chance on the sale gaining public attention. It is the job of the business broker to qualify potential buyers.

As a potential buyer, you need to be prepared to discuss with your business broker the details of your financial status and financing capabilities. However, in certain circumstances, depending on the seller's requirements, a seller will carry some financing, so just a statement of personal net worth may not be the only thing that makes someone a qualified buyer. The business broker will have a good idea of the seller's requirements, both monetarily and subjectively.

A good example is an aging seller preparing to exit the business who may be looking for a capable buyer to learn the business and eventually take over the business. So, it is important to be able to express to your broker not only your financial status but also your goals, abilities, and relevant history.

14. Review the business's financial statements.

Normally, the next step in the process, before approaching the owner through your broker, is to review the operating and balance sheets for the business. As explained, these financials are usually not audited statements and may not present an "accurate" financial picture. But they are better than nothing. Ideally, there should be at least the last three years of financials to review.

Things to look for in the financials:

Operating Statement (P&L)

The broker should have asked that the seller identify particular expense items that are considered part of the total return to ownership. However, at the inception of the due diligence process, sellers may be reluctant to identify these items without a signed non-disclosure agreement in place first. Here are some items to look for within the P&L statements:

a. Revenue trends over the years.

b. EBITDA trend (net operating profit before interest, taxes, depreciation, and amortization)

c. COGS trend (Cost of Goods Sold)

d. Operating expense trend

e. Note any deviations from the norm

f. Look at a detailed version of the P&L to review individual expense line items

g. Ask for a record of the latest year's state sales tax paid report

Balance Sheet:

a. Current ratio (current assets divided by current liabilities)

b. Long-term liabilities

c. Total assets

d. Equity trend

e. Determine how much debt is outstanding and to whom it is owed

Other related documents:

a. Most current cash flow

b. Vendor list

c. Most recent business valuation

15. Research company marketing programs.

Look at advertising and marketing costs and find out what programs have been the most effective (in terms of ROI).

16. Review the equipment list.

Note the amount of depreciation taken on the equipment. Later in the process, you will need to identify the equipment that is still functional and not in need of replacement. In transactions that include a sizeable amount of equipment and machinery, a certified appraiser may be needed to appraise the value of those assets.

17. Does the business own the building and property?

a. If owned, what was the latest appraisal and can the loan be assumed?

b. If leased, when will the lease expire and can it be assumed?

18. Request the organizational chart and key staff's business-related bios.

An important consideration in the sale and purchase of a business is how the employees might react to a new owner; this is particularly true with key staff. If and when the transaction reaches a certain point, the owner's opinion about "potential desertion" should be solicited.

Also, most buyers will ask that the seller or key operational staff stay on during a period of transition. Indeed, if the buyer is not experienced in the business, it is not unusual that the buyer requires the seller or key staff to stay on for a defined period.

19. Develop a SWOT analysis.

The potential buyer should probe deeply into the pros and cons of the business by developing a list of observations that describe the strengths, weaknesses, opportunities, and threats (SWOT) to the business before making the initial offer.

Once the broker has determined that the potential buyer has enough information to decide whether to proceed deeper into a possible transaction, the broker can begin the negotiation process. Usually, this starts with a formal offer including an Earnest Money Deposit. This offer signifies to the seller that there is a serious buyer.

At this point, the potential buyer will need to have an idea of the value of the business and how much to offer as a starting offer price. The offer requires that the seller be willing to share more confidential information with the potential buyer. The business broker can play an important part, as most opening offers are not what the seller wants. The broker knows enough about the buyer to help hedge the offer by pointing out the possibility for negotiation and mutual benefits. Usually, at this point, the broker can bring buyers and sellers together offsite to initiate a question-and-answer period. However, the broker should be present to help provide third-party observations post-meeting.

20. Start negotiations.

The negotiation phase is where your business broker becomes a central player and can help make things happen while the buyer stays on the sidelines and develops a clear idea of what is needed to reach an agreement.

Some people may say that the broker has a conflict because they also have a desire to push the sale through. It is up to you as the buyer to make it clear to your broker what you will accept, and don't be afraid to walk away if it doesn't meet your criteria. There is always another opportunity.

Chapter 5

Valuation of a Business

The true valuation of a business is what the buyer is willing to pay and what the seller is willing to accept. Financial valuations and expert market analysis can only play a benchmarking role in the price negotiation process.

There are many ways to develop a valuation of a business. Which method is best depends mainly on the type of business. There are basically two types of businesses that make a clear line between financial industry analysis methods:

1) Companies that require expensive assets, such as machinery, and require a substantial investment in inventory; and

2) Service companies that do not require a heavy investment in capital equipment. As most smaller companies are service-oriented due to the lower investment in capital equipment, these companies do require substantial investment in people. But staffing is not usually part of the financial equation for business valuation.

For businesses that are capital asset intensive, equipment value plays an important part in valuation and usually requires a certified appraisal to determine the equipment value. On the other hand, service businesses place much more importance on the asset of cash flow generated from operations as well as growth rates.

In both cases, buyers are interested in assuring future cash flows, usually based on the proforma operational forecasts for a specified period. Indeed, forecasting is a dicey undertaking and depends heavily on assumptions such as revenue and expense growth rates. No one has a crystal ball, but the buyer will need to determine whether the forecast estimates are reasonable or not.

This is where the negotiation process comes into play, and it usually starts with an "established" benchmark price. One must be aware that many industries come up with what they consider industry anecdotal "multiples" based on prior sales of businesses in the industry. However, when seeking capital, most valuation methods follow standard financial industry methods.

There are three main methods for valuing a business.

1. Asset-Based Method

The asset-based method looks at the business's assets and liabilities and the calculation is the difference between assets and liabilities.

Book value is the number shown as "owner's equity" on the balance sheet.[7] Book value is not a very useful number, since the balance sheet reflects historical costs and depreciation of assets rather than their current market value.

---

[7] Wolters Kluwer. "Best Business Valuation Formula for Your Business." Bizfilings.com. https://www.bizfilings.com/toolkit/research-topics/running-your-business/exit-strategies/use-the-best-business-valuation-formula-for-your-business (accessed February 16, 2020).

However, if you adjust the book value in the process of recasting your financials, the current adjusted book value can be used as a "bare minimum" price for your business.

Liquidation value is the amount that would be left over if you had to sell your business quickly—without taking the time to get the full market value—and then use the proceeds to pay off all debts. There's little point in going through all the trouble of negotiating a sale of your business if you end up selling for liquidation value—it would be easier to simply go out of business, and save yourself the time, broker's commission, attorney's fees, and other costs involved in selling a going concern. Thus, liquidation value is not even considered a valid floor for the price of your business (and you can use this argument in negotiations if you get an offer that approaches liquidation value).

Asset-based valuation is a balance sheet-based approach that is relied upon most often for companies generating losses (or only modest levels of income in relation to their net assets).

2. Market Method

The market method compares a business to similar companies that have already sold, and the business value is dependent on the local marketplace.

The market method offers an amount close to the fair market value. Fair market value means your small business net worth is what buyers are willing to pay. You must increase or decrease your business's price, depending on what buyers will pay.

Taking a market approach to valuing a business means identifying similar businesses and their recent sales prices. As a popular method for valuing home prices, it can be useful for businesses where a large amount of data on recent sales exists. It can be used in conjunction with one or more other methods to determine an accurate value.

Market-Based Key Data Points[8]

Being able to compare sales prices is only the beginning. In terms of valuing a home, key data points would include things like square footage and the number of bedrooms and bathrooms. When valuing a business, look for similar businesses by industry, location, number of employees, annual revenue, and other factors. It may also be useful to use a figure such as the EBITDA multiple to compare the relative financial strength of each business.

Market-Based Drawbacks

One major drawback of the market-based approach is that it is overly reliant on data, and the quality and quantity of that data is often not sufficient, particularly when valuing small businesses. While a market-based approach may work very well when comparing businesses with a high percentage of commercial real estate assets, it is less likely to yield accurate results when comparing small businesses with a large number of intangible assets.

3. Market Multiple Valuation Method

Market multiples are ways to compare similar companies as to performance and sale price. Normally, public companies, which are required to have third-party audited financial

---

[8] Newcomer-Dyer, Robert. "How to Value a Business: The Ultimate Guide for 2020." Fit Small Business. https://fitsmallbusiness.com/how-to-value-a-business/ (accessed February 16, 2020).

statements, use market multiple valuations; however, for smaller, non-public companies, these financial ratios are not easily found, but they do exist.

Seller's discretionary cash flow (SDCF), also known as seller discretionary earnings (SDE) or adjusted net, is a common cash flow-based measure of business earnings for owner-operator managed businesses. Value under the SDCF method can be determined as follows:[9]

- Start with the business's EBITDA earnings.

- Add business-related non-operating expenses and subtract non-operating income.

- Add unusual or one-time expenses, subtract non-recurring income.

- Add depreciation and amortization expenses.

- Add interest expenses, subtract interest income.

- Add a single owner's total compensation.

- Add compensation of all other business owners.

Transactions then use the resultant number as a base valuation and then add such things as "goodwill" and other non-financial assets like a book of customers, local brand, growth rate, and what is happening in the industry to arrive at a negotiated value.

---

[9] ValuAdder. "Seller's Discretionary Cash Flow."
https://www.valuadder.com/glossary/sdcf.html (accessed February 16, 2020).

Pick your multiple[10] – If your company is growing, potential buyers or investors will pay more than $1 per $1 of your earnings. For small businesses, the range is often between 0 and 4. If you have discretionary earnings of $100,000 and you believe that you deserve a multiple of 1.5, your intangible assets have an estimated value of $150,000.

There are services that provide a reference "multiple" for specific industries. Examples include www.peercomps.com, www.bizcomps.com, and www.valusource.com.

Most small company financials offered by sellers are not audited, so many buyers prefer to use the market multiple based on revenue, which can be easier to verify. Simply put, the revenue or EBITDA is multiplied by the market multiple to produce a valuation. Of course, there are many other factors to be considered when valuing a business, and that makes using market multiples only an approximate benchmark number to consider.

Add net liquid assets – What would your business have left after paying off all debt? This would include all cash, stock, bonds, real estate, and equipment. Add the total value of your net liquid assets to the figure you calculated in Step 2. If you have net liquid assets of $75,000, the total value of your business is $225,000.

You may have noticed that much of what constitutes valuation is based on what you "think." You may think last year's banner earnings were a sign of things to come. An investor might want to look at the average over three to five

---

[10] Parker, Tim. "Ways to Calculate the Value of a Small Business." Business Know-How. https://www.businessknowhow.com/money/calculatevalue.htm (accessed February 16, 2020).

years. You might think that you deserve a multiple of 2, but a buyer might only see a 1.5.

If you are placing value on your own business, think conservatively. Just as you have personal assets with sentimental value, you'll be tempted to add some "sweat equity" into the valuation.

If you ever negotiate with an investor or buyer, know that you'll likely have to negotiate. They probably won't pay 100 percent of its value, and the value might be lower than you believe.

Professional business appraisers and valuation experts may use a range of methodologies to determine a value, but those are merely indications meant for valuation comparison. **Ultimately, the actual value of a company depends on what the seller and buyer agree on and the amount of money that actually changes hands**. And this is what makes buying or selling a business a highly complex transaction and another reason to have a professional provide guidance and support. Indeed, just agreeing to a price leads into the contract that protects both buyer and seller for potential errors or omissions.

Just imagine how a For Sale by Owner (FSBO) transaction can run amuck, intentionally or unintentionally. If the buyer or seller is not familiar with the due diligence that should be performed, both parties can be hurt and lawyers reap the benefits. Buying a business is not like buying anything else. It can be a life-changing event and should be undertaken with careful consideration.

Negotiation Stage

The key to any negotiation is defining what both parties require to satisfy their needs and expectations. Discovering those needs and expectations requires an honest dialogue. But, naturally, both parties want to get the best deal they can for themselves.

Here is a fact to consider when speaking about negotiations. If both parties are bargaining together directly, it makes it more difficult to reach a compromise. Egos can get in the way. It is preferred to have a third party who understands the needs of both parties and tries to facilitate a compromise that satisfies everyone. Using a third-party negotiator allows both decision-makers to speak openly through independent "shuttle diplomacy." That said, not everybody is a good negotiator, which is a very important factor to consider when choosing your business broker.

FIGURE 3: NO. 1 REASON BUSINESSES DON'T SELL

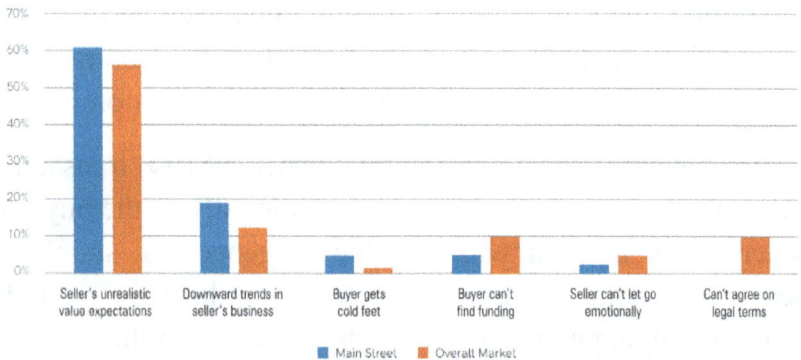

Figure 4. Graph showing top reasons why businesses don't sell. International Business Brokers Association. "Market Pulse Q3 2019." Accessed February 16, 2020. https://www.ibba.org/wp-content/uploads/2019/11/MarketPulse_Q3_2019_ExecutiveSummary.pdf

Things to Look for When Choosing a Business Broker

When interviewing a broker, make sure you are not just conversing with the company representative. It is imperative that you are speaking and interacting with the actual person who will represent you in the transaction, particularly your representative during the negotiating phase. Here are some recommended questions to ask during business broker interviews:

How much experience do you have selling businesses like mine?

No one person can know everything about the business world, but someone who has not only experience as a business owner but is also actually trained in the transactional process is particularly important when buying or selling a business. In many states, there are no specific requirements to become a business broker. However, in states such as Nevada, business brokers are required to be licensed and permitted.

The broker should be familiar with how the particular business operates, what is happening in the industry, and what is happening in the local market. Of particular importance is understanding the key operational aspects of the business and what the risks might be. On the buying side of the transaction, clients should ask the broker if they know why the seller is placing their business on the market and whether they have had the opportunity to meet with the seller to gain an understanding of their motivations to sell.

Do you work from home or in an office?

There is nothing wrong with working from home, and many companies are migrating to a virtual environment to cut costs. When it comes to business brokers, though, working from home will sometimes signify that this is not the individual's full-time occupation. The last thing you want to do is hire a broker who isn't going to give your listing his or her full attention because they have another job that might take up the majority of their time.

A business brokerage with an office typically means that they have a full team of brokers that will work towards reaching the buy or sell goals of their clients with the support of a team of experts. An office setting also presents a professional environment to handle negotiations and meet with potential sellers and buyers. The broker you choose to hire is a direct representation of your business interest.

Does dual agency provide the best outcome for buyers and sellers?

If a broker represents both sides of a transaction, there is a potential conflict of interest. Both sellers and buyers need to be aware of this potential conflict during the process and consider that in their working relationship with the broker. The reality for a broker is that they only get paid when a transaction has been successfully completed. Most brokers understand that both parties need to be satisfied to reach a deal. Indeed, the broker's interest should be secondary to facilitating the transaction on behalf of both parties.

How do you value a business?

Asking a business broker how he or she values a business will give you a good indication of how experienced they are. If they give you a cookie-cutter response such as "net income multiplied by two" before trying to qualify the situation, then turn and run. Valuation calculations have so many factors to consider—the same formula doesn't work for every business. As a matter of fact, different industries can use different ways to calculate the value of a business.

How do you maintain confidentiality?

A competent broker will be able to stir up interest by providing teaser information. Once a potential buyer expresses interest, the broker will qualify the client to ensure they have the financial ability to purchase the business. Once qualified, the broker should have a signed non-disclosure agreement before releasing any sensitive details about the business. Maintaining confidentiality should be one of the broker's main objectives.

How many listings do you have at the moment?

A broker with a large number of listings might be taking on every listing they can in hopes that they will eventually sell one. The "throw it against the wall and see what sticks" approach is not an effective approach. Look for a business brokerage that has between three to seven active listings per broker. Of course, as with all businesses, there are cycles.

How do you approach negotiations?

Is the broker a good listener, or do they try to dominate the conversation? As discussed, most negotiators first concentrate on gaining an understanding of the temperament and needs of both sides. A "consultative sales technique" is where logical assumptions are developed that are built on accepted conditions that can benefit both parties. A good consultative sale requires no real hard closing techniques. It becomes a mutual, logical decision based on an agreement that is seen as a mutual benefit.

Do you help with sales contract preparation? Do I need an attorney?

An experienced broker should be able to assist with the drafting of legal agreements and should have experience with different ways to structure deals. That being said, they should also advise you to hire an independent legal team to review documents before they are signed.

Use your broker for the initial paperwork and structuring of the transaction, but always have it reviewed by business lawyers before you go to the signing table. With so many different county and state laws and regulations, you need to be certain that all of your T's are crossed, and I's dotted. The small legal expense can end up saving you headaches and money down the road.

Chapter 6

Closing the Deal and Final Thoughts

During the due diligence process, both sellers and buyers will know what each needs to do to ensure a smooth transition of ownership. Once the transaction has been completed, both former and new owners need to meet with key employees and inform them of what has taken place. During these confidential meetings, key staff should express their concerns and how they think the other rank and file employees will react to the change.

It is important to get key staff on board with the new owner as change is always threatening. Sending a "go it slow" message is usually the way to help nervous employees keep an open mind. Talking about making changes is not a good idea at the start. However, if possible, provide employees with a positive spin on what the change can mean for them.

Often, the new owner will want the ex-owner-operator and key staff to stay on for some time to ensure a smooth transition. **This stipulation needs to be specified in the purchase agreement**.

Another reason to keep the ex-owner close at hand, at least for a while, is because invoices incurred before the change of ownership will come to the new owner and need to be satisfied by the ex-owner. Also, having key staff around will help new managers learn all the idiosyncrasies of the daily operations and gain a better understanding about the capabilities of the staff.

Final Thoughts

Buying or selling a business is a complex transaction. Each business has its own culture, policies, procedures, challenges, opportunities, and local client profiles. The key to having a positive outcome is dependent on how the transaction is approached. For the seller, this is particularly important as the focus still needs to be on operating the business and not being distracted by the demands required of the sale process.

Sellers often view their business as "their child" or their tormentor or somewhere in between. As a result, there can be a strong emotional component that requires careful navigation. Owner-operators invest time and emotional capital in their employees and customers. Naturally, the transaction must satisfy any concern about the future well-being of these vested parties.

Buyers enter the transaction with excitement, exuberance, and caution. A broker who takes time to understand their buyer's capabilities and interest will provide critical perspective and clarity. Experience and objectivity should be the framework to balance dreams of riches with a fear of failure.

Whether you are an owner-operator considering the sale of your business or a potential buyer looking for an exciting opportunity, the use of this guidebook will prepare you for the complex process you are about to begin. By following the recommendations outlined throughout the book, you are sure to engage in a smooth and successful transaction of buying or selling a business.

About the Author

Larry Goldstein is a Las Vegas, Nevada-based business broker whose expertise includes business valuation, complex negotiations, and multi-channel marketing. As a former business owner who successfully grew and sold his own business, Larry provides the unique perspective of how buying and selling a business really works.

Armed with a B.S. in Electrical and Biomedical Engineering and an M.B.A. from the University of Southern California, Larry has always had an interest in how businesses operate. He spent more than 20 years working as a management, marketing, and sales professional for major companies in the telecommunications and information technology industries such as SBC Communications, IBM, Nextel, and Spirent.

In 2011, Larry set his sights on going into business for himself. He bought the Rapid Refill of Las Vegas franchise, providing customers fast and cost-effective printer supply solutions. In 2014, he purchased the entire local franchise operation to better serve customers by expanding the business to provide additional products and services and sold this business in 2016.

Seller Due Diligence Checklist

(pages 21-28)

☐ Analyze why you want to sell the business.

☐ Can you identify any fixes that can address why you feel the need to sell?

☐ What will you do once the business is sold?

☐ Thoroughly investigate your exit options before deciding to sell.

☐ Determine how to market the business for sale.

☐ Interview and choose a business broker.

☐ Create a sales brochure.

☐ Clean up the financial reports.

☐ Prepare point of sale records.

☐ Clean up the location, equipment, and operations.

☐ Gather all required operational documentation.

- [ ] Gather all employee handbooks, policies and procedures, training programs, and employee reviews.

- [ ] Obtain pre-sale finance options including SBA pre-approval.

- [ ] Engage with exit planning professionals.
    - CPA / tax expert
    - Wealth management advisors
    - Business transaction attorney

Buyer Due Diligence Checklist

(pages 29-40)

☐ Understand why you are looking to purchase a business rather than look for a job?

☐ If you know what type of business you wish to consider, research everything you can about the industry, its history, and its potential outlook.

☐ If you are not sure of what business you would be interested in, revisit your reasons for thinking about purchasing a business.

☐ Is your significant other ready for the type of commitment and potential risks of owning a business?

☐ Become familiar with key listing websites such as www.bizbuysell.com.

☐ Find out if the business has a sales memorandum.

☐ Check out the business' website, as well as local competitors.

☐ Google the business and a map of its location as well as the locations of nearby competitors.

☐ Research the local demographics.

- ☐ Contact related national business associations.

- ☐ Contact local Chamber of Commerce offices.

- ☐ Contact local business development offices.

- ☐ Engage with local business brokers

- ☐ Become familiar with the process.

- ☐ Qualify as a potential buyer – commercial financing, SBA, or seller carry back.

- ☐ Review the business's financial statements.

- ☐ Review company marketing programs.

- ☐ Review equipment list.

- ☐ Does the business own the building and property?

- ☐ Gather the organization chart and key staff's business-related bios.

- ☐ Develop a SWOT analysis.

- ☐ Start negotiations.

www.ingramcontent.com/pod-product-compliance
Lightning Source LLC
Chambersburg PA
CBHW060323220326
41598CB00027B/4409